The Stranger
is
My Friend

The Stranger is My Friend

Glocally Connected with Inlandia Books

I was a stranger in this land

Then you came closer

With open arms and a full plate

So now I take your hand

— Nikia Chaney

artwork by Christina Guillén

Foreword

Many voices from our community make up this collection. May these poems remind us to reach out, because the stranger may soon become our dear friend.

In these times of the pandemic, where we are forced to stay home and can't even be with our loved ones for the sake of their safety, we are once again reminded of the challenges refugees face every day. Sudden changes of life, longing to be with our loved ones, and helplessness that we cannot change our circumstances, are all part of the experience of being a refugee. Now more than ever, may we see how similar we all are to each other. May these works of art stand as a great reminder of that.

A heartfelt thank you goes out to Cati Porter, director of Inlandia Institute, who applied for and was awarded a Cultural Pathways grant from the California Arts Council. She has the unique talent of being a manager, facilitator and poet. She was with us for every step of the project and we are forever grateful for this partnership.

Nikia Chaney and Christina Guillén, facilitators and poets from Inlandia Institute, provided just enough guidance to ignite a sense of purpose in our writing. Some poetry was spoken in Pashto and Farsi and then written by a friend and lastly translated into English. Language was not a barrier nor was any training or education in writing poetry. There was no hesitation to create poetry; on the contrary, there was only enthusiasm.

Thank you to the SCIPP facilitators who joined us during the summer of 2019. In four sessions across the span of two weeks, art and poetry were created by the children. And in the adult ESL class, deeper and nuanced cultural understanding came through when we each shared the story of our favorite scarf.

Further support came from The Critical Refugee Study Collective grant that Zehra Qazi was awarded. Beautiful art projects were created that were built on the theme of community building. Thanks to this grant, a pre launch of this book happened in March 2020 where the Afghan women shared their art and poetry.

Glocally Connected is a volunteer-based organization and it would not continue to grow if it were not for the many volunteers who support our work and our families in every possible way from driving the women to class to supporting their entrepreneurial efforts; teaching in the classroom; opening their hearts; and building the bonds of friendship.

—Selin & Sherry

Dear Glocally Connected family,

I have cherished every moment of working on this book. I especially loved writing the poetry with the Afghan women and our volunteers. I would have never imagined that creating poetry would come more effortlessly from the students than myself or the volunteers. Perhaps it's because there's a strong oral tradition of poetry in Afghanistan or the fact that they were not caught up in the form but rather focused on the expression. In a poem that I composed for the students, I expressed how,

It just wasn't for you

It was for us

We all needed the purity

  Of expression

  That we learned from you

We became family

I was reminded of how healing it can be to share what's on our heart, especially with a friend.

—Sherry MacKay

UCR student Phong Hong, recipient of the Donald A Strauss Fellowship, helped develop a public health program to support the families from Glocally Connected, and initiated a refugee poetry contest for UCR students and our families. There were some beautiful poems entered and we include them here for your reading pleasure. All poetry contest entries are noted with an asterisk beside their title.

Contents

Home is a Place I Can Hang My Heart: Women's Writing and Art

Home is Where I Live:
Children's Writing and Art

A Bag Full of Oranges on Her Head:
Volunteers & Staff Contributions

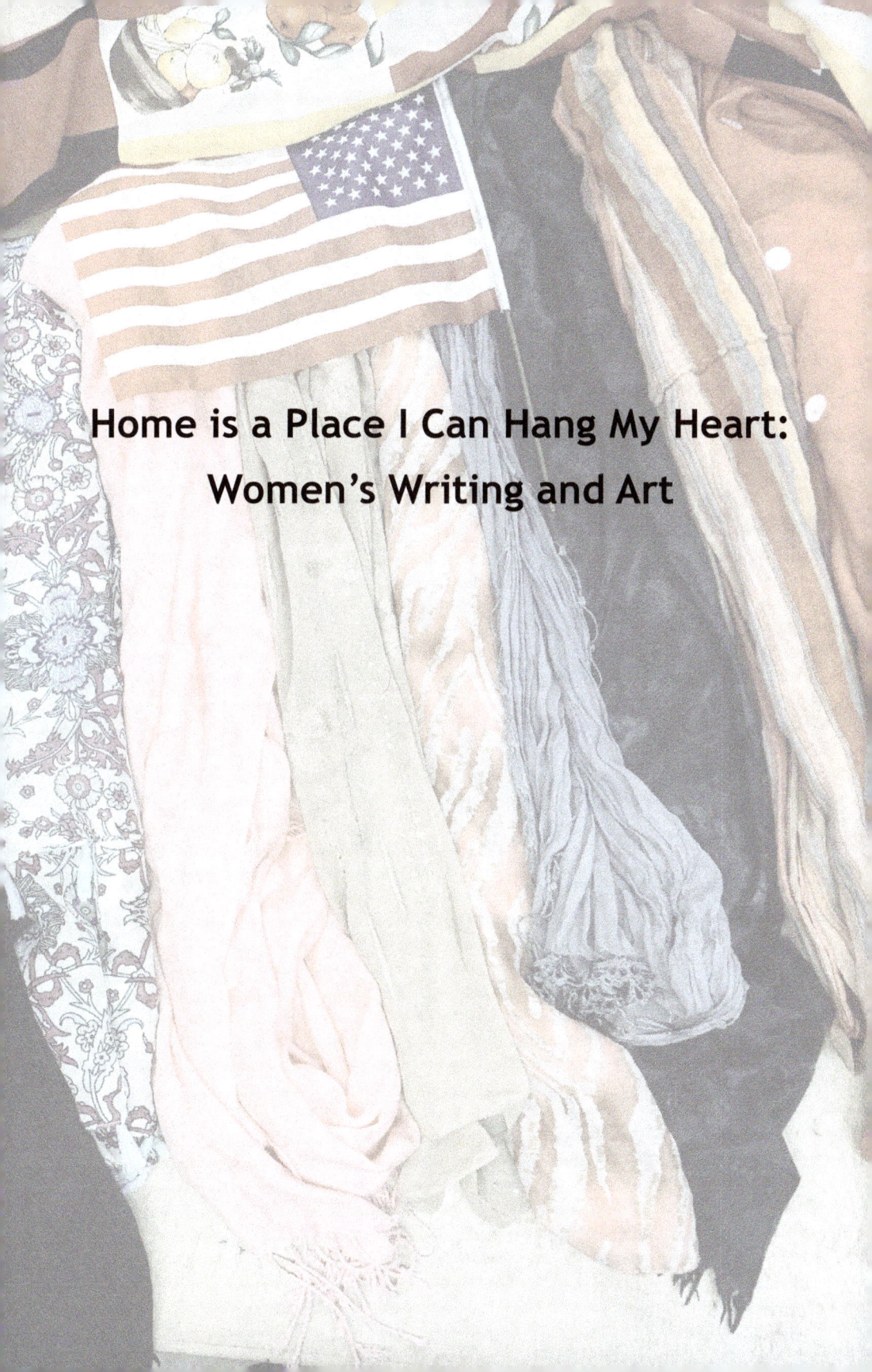

Home is a Place I Can Hang My Heart:
Women's Writing and Art

Khatira Kakar

I am very happy because
my family connection is LOVE

I am sad because my family is far away from me

Khadija Karwan

I enjoy my life with my husband and my children because I know that my children will grow up and this time is short.

Latifa, Shabnam, Zia, Friba

What do you want to share about America?

The place where you can dream

Living here is not what we feel

In this strange world a life

with no home

Homesick and sad with an empty heart

I roam

Searching for anyone to just

understand

But it is the stranger who makes

happiness...

she says "you are me and I am you"

Ziagul, Farishta, Nasreen, Adeela Mahboba, Famida

When I came to this strange country this strange place

Everyday I am so upset, the tears flow on my face

I miss my country and my family and my old home

My eyes stay red with crying, I feel so alone

When suddenly I think about how hard and difficult this all is

and a person appears in front of me just like this

and changes my sadness and makes my pain pass

and we come together in class and laugh and laugh and laugh

څه چه کله راغلم

کله چه څه راغلم دی نا اشنا ملک ته

ټوله ورځ به څه ناسته په ژړا وم

دا دیده به راته خپل او پردی واړه

تل به سری سترگی څه ناسته په ژړا وم

ناڅاپه ناست وم یوه ورځ ډوبه فکرونو کی

راغلو راته مخکی یو نفر حیرانوونکی وو

بدل می شول دردونه او فکرونه ټول

راغلو مونږ دی کلاس په خندا شو ټول

Latifa Badrey

Hope

Hope Peace Healthy.

I believe in my God because my God is everywhere, my job, my life, my family.

Give more love to our group.

I hope for kindness for my children.

Next year I want us to learn more English. I want to understand more English. Write more English.

I want to laugh more.

Mahboba Shirzad

About my grandmother

She is very good and she is so kind, which I can't explain. When I was small, she showed me good ways of living. She helped me in my education by providing clothes and other things. I wish her a great and happy life but now she has a lot of problems because of the economic crisis and war. I pray to God for her health and happiness every night. God bless her in both worlds.

محبوبه

در باره مادرکلانم

مادرکلانم بسیار زن خوب و مهربان است, من نمیتوانم تشریح کنم. من که کوچک بودم راه راهی بهتر زندگی را برایم یاد میداد. مرا در مکتب و درس هایم کمک میکرد, برایم لباس و وسایل مکتب تهیه میکرد. من برایش دعا میکنم و ارزوی زندگی خوب برایش میکنم, فعلاً در شرایط مشکل قرار دارد, جنگ است و وضیعت اقتصادی خراب دارند.

من از هر شب به الله متعال برای صحت, سلامتی و زندگی آرام برایش دعا میکنم.

الله متعال او را در هر دو دنیا مورد رحمت خود قرار بدهد.

Mahboba Shirzad

I am strong and hard working

I wonder when I start college

I hear studying holy Quran

I see my children graduating

I want to help with orphans

I am strong and hard working

I pretend I am a teacher of my children

I feel happy when my children read the Quran

I touch Makah

I worry about my children's future

I try to teach my children Islamic subject

I dream peace in Afghanistan

I hope my sons will get married and have children

I am strong and hard working

Scan the QR code on your mobile device to hear an audio recording of this poem on Soundcloud.

Mahboba Shirzad

When we are together at home
I feel so happy and quiet

When my children are studying the Quran
I feel lucky and peaceful

When my son Tawheed Ullah is studying
books I am so happy

I hope my children
will become good men
in the future

InshaAllah

artwork by Mahboba Shirzad

Farishta Sherzad

About My Grandmother

My dear grandmother taught me everything. She taught me how to think right and be wise. She taught me the difference between bad and good. She taught me how to be kind. She helped me through my education by taking me to school and providing clothes and other things. I pray to God for her health and happiness every night. God bless her in both worlds.

فرشته

در مورد مادرکلانم

مادرکلان عزیزم همه چیز را برایم یاد میداد. او برایم یاد میداد که چطور درست و عاقلانه فکر کنم. او فرق میان خوب و بد را برایم یاد میداد. برایم یاد میداد که چطور مهربان باشم. او مرا در تعلیم و تربیه ام کمک میکرد، مرا به مکتب میبرد برایم لباس و دیگر لوازم میخرید. من هرشب برای صحت و خوشی ها برای مادر کلانم دعا میکنم, الله متعال وی را در دنیا و اخرت مورد رحمت خود قرار دهد.

Farishta Sherzad

I feel so happy in my home
When I touch my kids
I feel I am a lucky mom
because my Allah gave me
children like angels

Tahmina Noori

I hope to become a citizen.

I hope to speak better English.

I hope my daughters will become doctors and my sons engineers.

I believe in God.

Tahmina Noori

I am Tahmina
I like my pink scarf because it is my favorite
color. This pink scarf
was a gift from my father when I left
my country for the U.S.

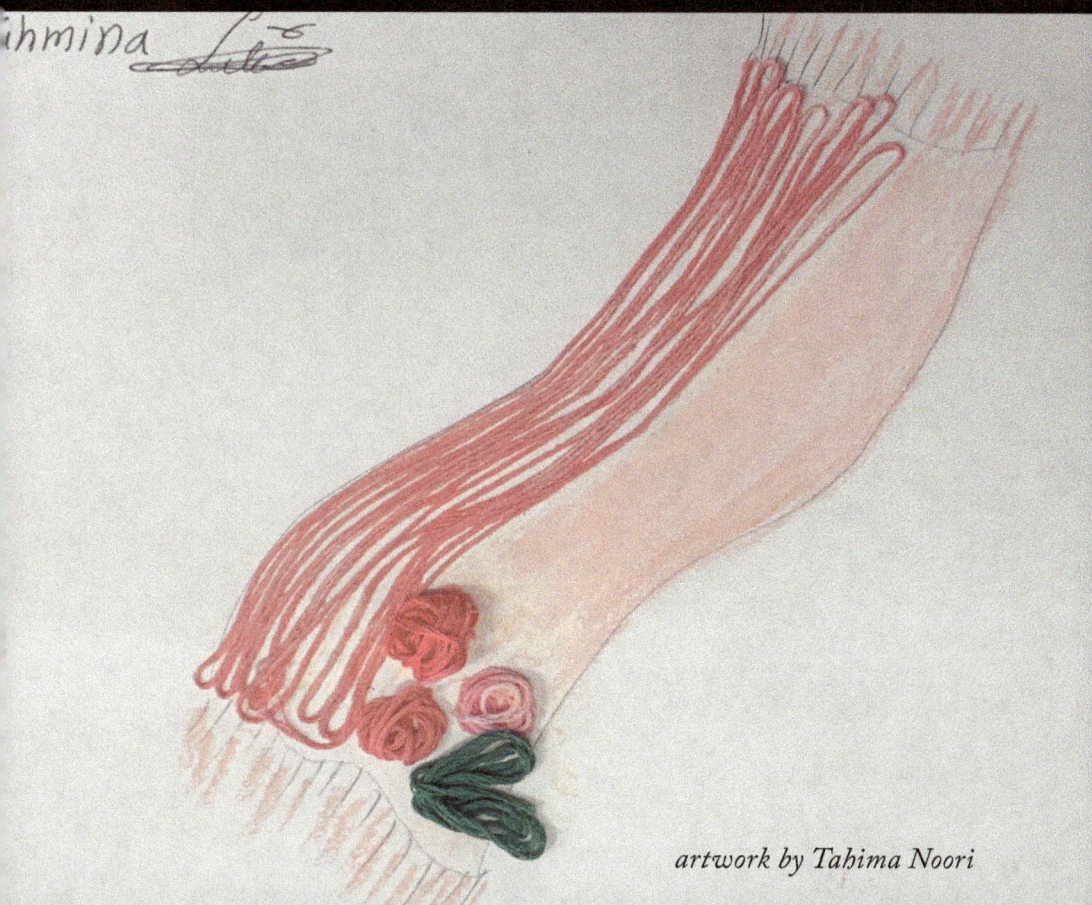

artwork by Tahima Noori

Tahmina Noori

I draw this because
I always think about good
   things.
I want to learn English and
   find a job in the future.
I hope I can reach my goal.

Sabrine Hossain*

His Dream

I remember my father coming
home one night
Blood weeping from an open
wound
He said nothing as my mother
tended to his forehead
His silence was louder than
her wailing

He had shaved his beard
Changed his name
Prayed at home instead of
the mosque
Continued to smile at strangers
even after they spat the word
terrorist in his face

All for a love for a country
that went violently unrequited
A country that would never let
him forget sins he did not commit

"This is the sacrifice we make for the
American dream," my father said
later on

I always wondered what could
be worth enduring this much
I didn't realize his dream was
actually me

* *refugee poetry contest entry*

Mesbah Dawar[*]

The Memories

Every part of our lives is a memory. The bad memories that we may never forget, and good memories that when they come into our minds make us feel calm. All of our memories are related to us, but remembering the good ones brings us happiness and peace when we are upset.

How can we have a good memory?

It is easy! Just chill your life. This world is nothing but a test that we are given from God. So, why we do not live it in a better way to make lasting memories?

Don't think about sadness, just be happy. Be yourself, think positive about your future, and deal with any risk in a constructive way and be strong.

Everyone has good and bad memories. I have both, but thank God my good memories outweigh my bad memories. My good memories are full of wonder with my family and my friends from back home. I really miss the days I had with my friends.

Twenty girls used to sit under the shade of a huge pine tree. Guess what we were doing there!

We were doing a lot of girly talks and chatting about our futures, we played truth or dare, sang and danced. We had a lot of fun. It took us far away from sadness and bad things that happen in the world, especially in my country.

Every memory is important. Some when we remember them make us happy. From some others we can learn new lessons, always try to keep good memories from every moment of your life. Good memories and remembering them makes us healthy, stay young, always happy, and makes your soul feel peaceful.

* *refugee poetry contest entry*

Friba Dawar*

Safe Place

If you want to be successful, start thinking positive and set your goals for yourself as a success.

I want to write about my travel memories. I want to share with you a few memories of my trip from Kabul to Riverside, CA.

A journey where I was looking for a safe and better life.

It was very difficult for me to leave my home, country, friends, and my career.

It was a big decision.

But I learned that no matter how much it hurts now, someday you will look back and realize your struggles changed your life to a better one.

I traveled.

I abandoned all.

In the new environment, I felt strange.

I felt like I was in the ocean, and I was not able to swim.

I felt pain. There are two types of pain in life, pain that hurts you and pain that changes you.

The only way I calmed down was to refer to Allah and pray.

He gives me energy, Thanks Allah.

I am empowered because I have a society which supports me...

Thank you friends...

Friba Dawar

Scarves for me have different meanings.

In different places wearing a scarf

people react different to me.

Like in Afghanistan I wear it for

safety and it is more

respectful.

But in U.S.A. it has a different feeling

I don't feel as safe

and sometimes I am scared.

I want to wear a scarf

because of my faith even

If it doesn't feel safe or comfortable.

Friba Dawar

I am faithful and brave

I wonder if someone will stop me

I hear peaceful sounds

I see blue color

I want to be strong

I am faithful and brave

I feel peace

I touch my father

I worry about injustice—inequality

I try to be respectful

I dream to be a leader

I hope I can reach my dream

I am faithful and brave

Friba Dawar

I draw a Jungle

I like to be free

like animals without judgment or darkness

I won't need to worry about the pains of life

Friba Dawar

Home is the warmth of life

In my home I feel the sweetness

I touch honesty and smell the happiness

Home is a place that I can hang my heart

artwork by Friba Dawar

Friba Dawar

Education dream
I wrote this poem on behalf of my friends

I dreamed a little dreams of me
Having a pen writing for me
In blue sky what I see
Having chance to read
And rainbow school come to me
But it was a dream just for me
I pray for it to come to me
He sends angels to me
To teach me …ABC…D

Fahmida Sadat

I am very sad because I

don't have sons

I have five daughters

My daughter asks why we don't

have a brother

my husband is also sad because

we have no son. In my

culture if the wife has no sons

her husband may get a new wife

I'm happy with my beautiful daughters

my story is very big—

I pray for my God to give me a son

Fahmida Sadat

Nasreen is good because she is a quiet and honest person.
She doesn't interfere in the life of anybody.

فهمیده

نسرین بسیار خوب است, او زن آرام و راستکار است. او در زندگی
هیچ کسی کار و دخالت نمیکند.

Fahmida Sadat

When I came in this country

I saw a tree like my

Hometown

I became excited and told my husband

Ooh! It is the same as the one in our village

Fahmida Sadat

I draw flowers because
I want peace and tranquility
in the world.
I wish I will have a beautiful life with
my family likes flowers.

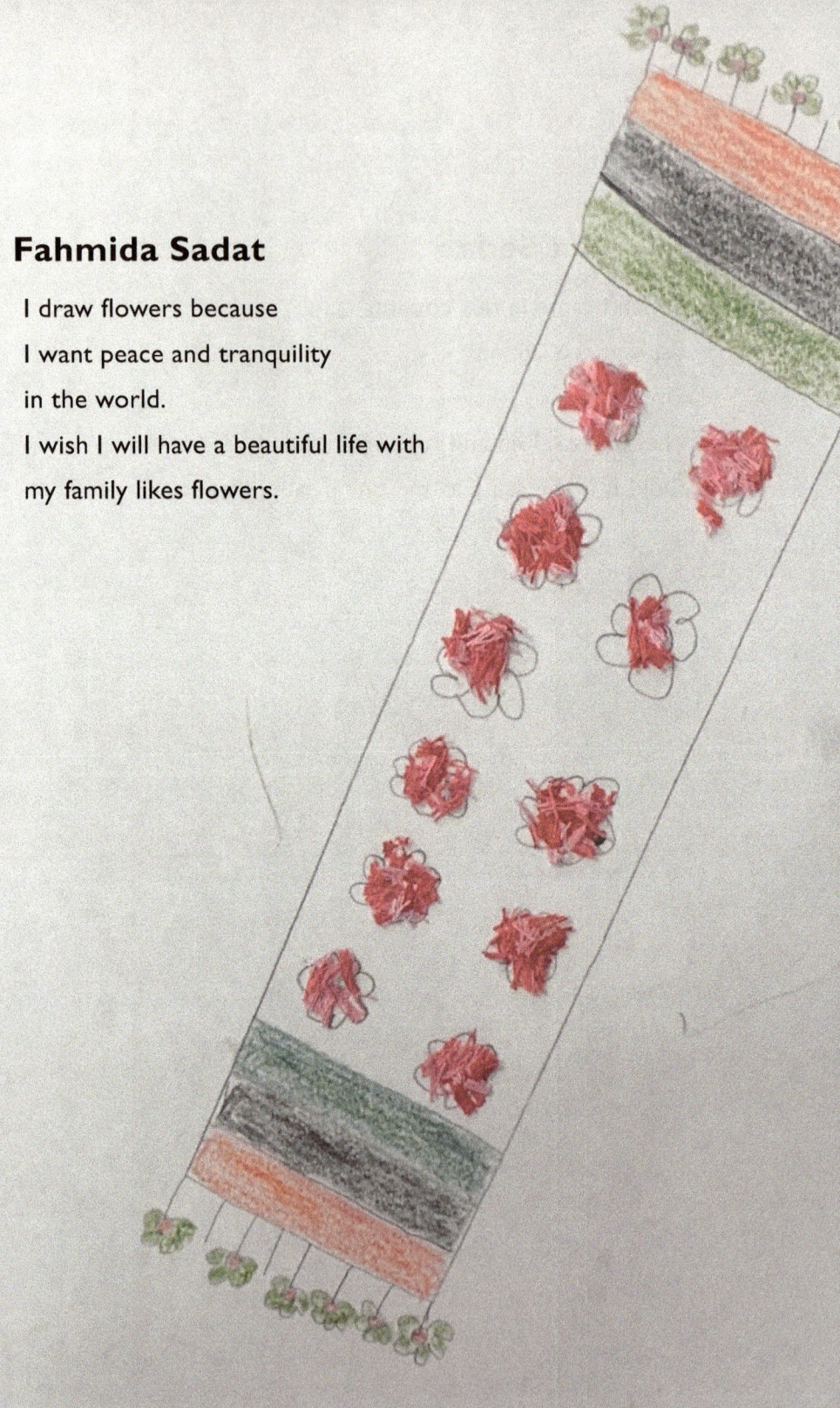

artwork by Fahmida Sadat

Shabnam Feraz

When I was a teen my mom advised me to learn cooking but I didn't pay attention to her. When I got married I faced a lot of challenges. There was no YouTube to learn from. I wished I listened to my mom.

شبنم

وقتیکه من نوجوان بودم مادرم برایم میگفت که باید آشپزی را یاد بگیرم ولی من هیچ توجه نمیکردم. زمانیکه عروسی کردم به بسیار مشکلات روبرو شدم. در آن وقت توتیوب نبود که از آن یاد میگرفتم, آرزو میکردم که کاش به گپ های مادرم گوش میکردم

Shabnam Feraz

I feel peace in my home
but sometimes, I miss my home.

Shabnam Feraz

I Am Poem

I am patient, kind

I wonder if I lost something

I hear quiet songs

I see a big house

I want to learn English

I am patient, kind

I pretend to be a teacher

I feel worry

I touch soft things

I worry about war

I try to be kind

I dream about a big house

I hope to go to the Hajj to pray

I am patient, kind

Shabnam Feraz

About Fawzia

She has a kind heart

She is smart

She is friendly

Her manner is so good

She makes me laugh

شبنم

در مورد فوزیه

او قلب مهربان دارد

او بسیار هوشیار است

او دوست خوب است

او رویه بسیار خوب دارد

او مرا میخنداند

Zahab Qazi*

Where I am From

I am from the place where two points meet, a culmination of
cultures.

Where the ocean on the west yearns to drown you whole,

Where the mountains of the east long to crush your soul be-
neath them.

It is neither here nor there, and yet

it follows me everywhere.

Where I am from you can hear the sound of the mauzzin beck-
oning you to prayer,

asking you to atone from a day of sins.

Where I am from the sound of freedom blares from radio and
nightclub, reassuring you that to truly find yourself,

you must first leave behind everything you have ever known.

Where I am from,

the rich smell of chili powder, turmeric, and mangoes and mint
invades the nose,

encasing you in an exotic,

but sometimes poisonous perfume.

Where I am from the only ceiling is the wide expanse of sky,
lined with rows of Hollywood palm trees,

sometimes it is a bolt of black velvet embedded with diamonds;

sometimes it is the clear honest blue of your lover's eyes,

or a fantastic burst of purples, blues and oranges as the sun
sinks into slumber,

other days it is a dismal, angry, stubborn haze of human incom-
petence.

Where I am from, the street peddler entices you
with the promise of perfectly roasted garbanzo beans
and freshly squeezed juice of lemons and oranges.

Where I am from,
the smell of death and poverty hides in the oxygen,
waiting patiently as you inhale its toxicity…
never realizing, never knowing…

Where I am from, a little girl cries for food that has no sub-
    stance or history,
for clothes that have been made in a faceless factory, made
    without patience or love
 and her mother slaps her across the face for her disobedience;
    but hidden from her daughter's eyes
she cries too.

Where I am from,
the grandmothers and aunts always worry about your marriage
and how well you make roti's,
but never wonder of your mind, only your body and its ability
    to bear children.
Where I am from your mother looks on,
the swallowed sorrow of dreams gone, welling in her eyes.

Where I am from you yearn for a name that rolls smoothly, and
    without hesitation from the white man's lips,
a cookie cutter name for those whose success is guaranteed,
A name without hope or struggle or meaning.

Where I am from you must be strong…
because life is always going
on.

Fawzia Azad

One day my mom's cousin was trying to teach us how to sew and we were all girls without scarves and the Taliban were going to come because they wanted to know why we didn't have scarves and what happened and they all hit the girls and my mom's cousin wanted to say, "Wait, let me put my scarf on my head," in Poshto, but she said, "Wait let me put my shoes on my head." The Taliban laughed and they didn't hit her because she didn't understand.

*Under constant surveillance by the Taliban, women in Afghanistan are required to wear head scarves. Fawzia never liked to wear scarves.

Fawzia Azad

I Am Poem

I am strong and brave

I wonder how I can help people

I hear waterfalls in morning

I see people laughing

I want a business

I am strong and brave

I pretend I have a business

I feel happy in my class

I touch a flower

I worry that I won't see my mom

I try to learn English

I dream to see my mom

I hope for world peace

I am strong and brave

Scan the QR code on your mobile device to hear an audio recording of this poem on Soundcloud.

Fawzia Azad

About Shabnam

Friends for one year
She smiles all the time
She is beautiful
The possibilities are good
Her words are good
Her heart is good
She is friendly
Her personality is good

فوزیه

درمورد شبنم

دوست از یکسال بدینسو
او همیشه لبخند بر لب دارد
او مقبول است

گپ هایش خوب است
قلب اش خوب است
بسیار دوست خوب است
شخصیت اش بسیار خوب است

Fawzia Azad

I want to be a seamstress
and help people have
beautiful dresses

I want to have a beautiful
garden in the future and have
fun with family

artwork by Sherry MacKay

Fawzia Azad

I hope for good health and healthy children. I hope to get my citizenship in 2020 and a job. I believe that God provides for me and takes care of me.

I hope for all people to live in peace with each other. No more wars, especially in Afghanistan.

Paulette Bruggeman

Home is green, quiet
with four seasons

Cool and fresh and clean
Dew drops on the leaves in the morning

Shower peace, no hustle bustle
peaceful, closer to God

Hearing my thoughts, calm
Feeling complete

Maple leaves are home
Ohio

Paulette Bruggeman

I believe that if we can accept each other, despite our differences, peace will be the result.

Felice Pope

Home is an illusion of the past.

A feeling of love, family,

talking at meals.

Hugs and kisses.

Unconditional love.

That is the past.

Neghena Hamidi*

Easy on their tongues

my mother assimilated when she limited our names to two
    syllables.

"It'll be easier on their tongues"

their tongues

easier so they don't remember you

easier on us so we don't have to explain to them the origins
    of our names

we assimilated when we started to answer to our nicknames

water lilies become diluted

as nilofar becomes nilo

call me whatever you want

your slave

your prostitute

negina to nicki

zarlasht to just zee

ferida to fairy

gem stones to flowers

a long journey to settle

with our names to cut up

in pieces to be powerless

although my name is beautiful

enough to flaunt

i assimilated when i told you my name rhymes with your
    mother's

only with a long e

and short u

i assimilated

my mother assimilated

we did

it started with our names

the beginning of our identities

only to rhyme like your mother's

but to still be seen as the other

~Child of Immigrants

refugee poetry contest entry

Susan Ismael*

Untitled

The strong and powerful

In our world, life seems so dark.
We've tasted the bitter dirt.
Someone told us that there was light.
But it was far from our desert.

The land of the free, they say.
The people are kind.
You can be wealthy and raise a family.
Opportunity is endless to find.

We travelled so far and wide,
So our family could have chances.
They say that in the United States
Our children won't worry about finances.

We trekked over the border,
We sacrificed our lives,
We were starved and tired,
But we ultimately survived.

But then there was 9/11 and
Life was harder than ever.
Islamophobia was everywhere
And the Muslim name was scarred forever.

We feared for our life,

And we feared for our children.

Wherever we were

We had to stay hidden.

Our dreams were fading,

Our opportunities were leaving.

We struggled in society

And our goals started to lose meaning.

But, then we remembered Allah.

He says we must not lose courage or patience,

We must keep our strength

And continue with motivation.

Our children are born strong

They succeed despite their situation.

They are the future leaders of the world

And are leaders in education.

We have shown strength,

We have shown endurance,

We have shown courage,

And we have shown resilience.

Adila Sadat

I wear a scarf because my

God becomes happy.

I feel comfortable and I like it.

I wear a scarf because my

God becomes happy.

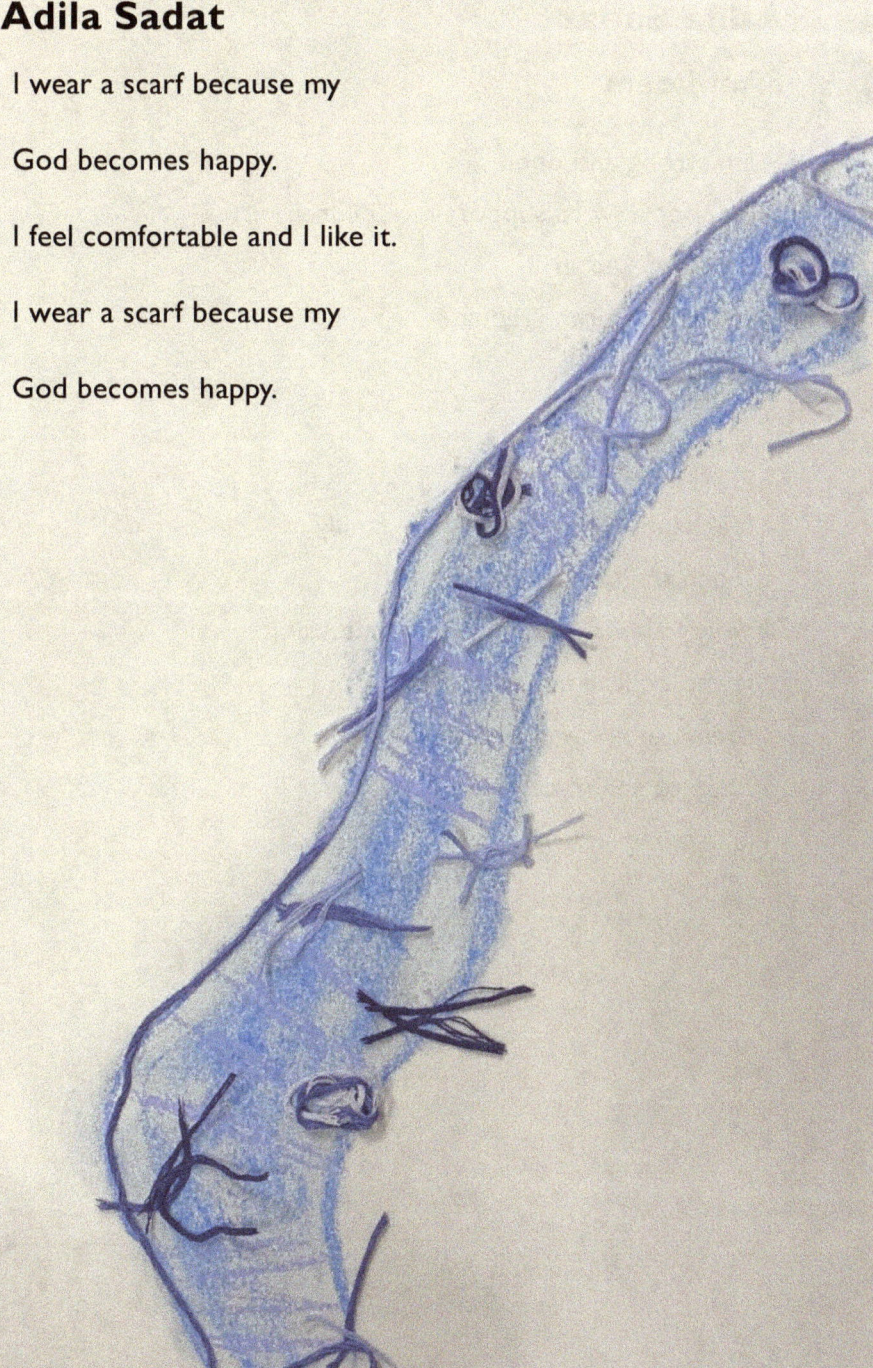

artwork by Jessie Godin

Adila Sadat

I Am Poem

I am strong and open

I wonder how to support my children

I hear the Quran

I see my children graduate

I want a house

I am strong and open

I pretend I am a bird

I feel happy when I see all my family

I touch the skin of my baby

I worry about my family in Afghanistan

I try to believe in happiness

I dream of always being here

I hope to see myself rich

I am strong and open

Adila Sadat

When me and my children sit together

I feel happy and relaxed

When Sara gives me a hug

I feel good smell

and I am so happy because my daughters finish school soon

Zia Sakhi

Hope

 I hope to be a good grandmother to my grandchildren—to support them—to provide babysitting for my eight grandchildren.

 I hope to help people, to be nice to everybody, to my class, to my teachers: Sherry, Julie, Norette, Suha, Mona, and the child caregivers, Sam and Shawnee.

 I believe in God; I pray five times a day; I believe the Quran. I am nice to everybody. I am happy and friendly to everyone in the class.

 I want to share with others—good food for everybody, and coffee and tea for everybody. I share with my American friends how to cook Afghani food.

artwork by Zia Sakhi

Zia Sakhi

I wear my scarf for my culture.
I feel good when I do not
wear it all the time. I show

my face. My husband says I
don't have to wear a scarf.
Now I wear in Mosque and
choose when I wear.
My daughter chooses not to wear scarves.
My kids say, "Mom don't wear a
scarf."

When I get a family picture
I wear a scarf around my
neck, not over my head or
face.

I am happy I do not have
to wear a burka anymore.

Zia Sakhi

About Sherry

Three years ago I found this school

I'm happy for Sherry

For everyone who is sad

Her heart is good for everyone

This school

I sit in my house

I don't go anywhere

For two days

I'm happy to see Sherry, my friend

I'm happy

ضیا

در مورد شیری

سه سال قبل من این مکتب را یافتم

من برای شیری بسیار خوشحال هستم

برای هر کس که غمگین میباشد،

قلب او برای همگی خوب است

این مکتب

من در خانه می نشینم

هیچ جای نمی روم

برای دو روز

من بسیار خوش میشویم که دوست خود شیری را میبینم

من خوش استم

Zia Sakhi

I have very good memories from my father. He used to come home smiling and he always provided for all of my needs. God bless him.

ضیا سخی

مه خاطرات بسیار خوش از پدرم دارم, وقتیکه به خانه میامد لبخند برلب داشت، هرچیز که میخواستم او برایم آماده میساخت. الله متعال رحمت اش کند.

Ziagul Shirzad

I feel by wearing a scarf
my God is happy with me.
I like it because I feel
comfortable. It is my culture.

Ziagul Shirzad

Latifa is a very good woman, because she has a very kind and lovely heart.

ضیاگل

لطیفه زن بسیار خوب است، بخاطر ایکه قلباً بسیار مهربان و دوست داشتنی است

Ziagul Shirzad

I feel so happy in my home.

When Masihullah calls me mommy

I feel all the world is mine.

I feel lucky that all my family is with me.

artwork by Ziagul Shirzad

Ziagul Shirzad

I want to have a pretty house in
the future. My house will have a
flower garden and I will have a happy
life with my family.

Ziagul Shirzad

My Family

My mother is a strong woman. She gave birth to twelve children. I love my mom. She loves us all and supports my disabled brothers. She was very kind in everything she taught me. I miss my mom. When I was little and I was playing in the yard, she said, "Come home," I liked that word, "home."

ضیاگل

فامیل من

مادرم یک زن بسیار قوی است, او دوازه اولاد به دنیا اورده. من مادرم را بسیار دوست دارم. او همه ما را بسیار دوست دارد و برادران معیوب ما را پرستاری میکند. او بسیار مهربان است, هرچیز را ما یاد میداد. پشت مادرم بسیار دق شده ام. وقتیکه خورد بودم و در حویلی بازی میکردم او صدایم میکرد «خانه بیا» من آن کلمات وی را بسیار دوست دارم

Ziagul Shirzad

I Am Poem

I am a kind woman and I want to be kind with other people

I worried about when I lost something

When I hear music or Quran I feel happy

I saw my bright future of my kids

I want to have a big garden full of different foods

I am a kind woman

If I had school in the past I would study and become a
teacher like my sister-in-law

I feel relaxed when I drive, I want to be a bus driver

I want to touch my parents

I worry about my son's future

I wish I could go back to my country

I dream about peace in Afghanistan

I hope my son's future becomes good and that he has a
bright future

I am so kind

*Scan the QR code on your mobile device to hear an audio
recording of this poem on Soundcloud.*

Marzia Sadat

I Am Poem

I am friendly and smart

I wonder how I will do in my college

I hear music

I see myself graduating

I want a car

I am friendly and smart

I pretend I'm an angel

I feel sad when people are fighting

I touch the money that I will make in my future

I worry about my country

I try to believe in honesty

I dream of going to my home country

I hope to see my brother's wedding

I am friendly and smart

Scan the QR code on your mobile device to hear an audio recording of this poem on Soundcloud.

Nasreen Shirzad

I hope God will give me nice kids in the future.

I believe in God, when I am sad and I have problems I pray to God because only God can better everything.

I want to share with everybody when I know some good things about health, cooking, clothes designing, and I also share my hope and my feelings with friends.

Nasreen Shirzad

My home is in need of my children's
sound. I feel sad because I
didn't have children. I love my
home. My husband and I feel safe
and relaxed in our home
I am very happy I started my
studying. Now I feel strong.
My home is my world.

Nasreen Shirzad

Fahmeda is a good woman because she has a good and honest heart. Her thinking is good.

نسرین

فهمیده زن بسیار خوب است، بخاطر ایکه او قلب بسیار پاک و صادق دارد. او بسیار خوب فکر میکند

Nasreen Shirzad

I Am Poem

I am kind and honest and creative

I wonder about my family

I hear Sora and Alrahman and it makes me feel relaxed

I see my children playing

I want my own business

I am kind and honest

I pretend to be a journalist

I feel hopeful that I have a happy family

I touch my children's face

I worry about people fighting

I try to be honest

I dream about having my non-profit

I hope to be happy and successful

I am kind and honest

Scan the QR code on your mobile device to hear an audio recording of this poem on Soundcloud.

Nasreen Shirzad

My Family

My mother is a strong and very kind woman. She bore eight children. She loves and cares for us all. When I was little my mom said, "Don't say anything false in your life because that is very bad for your personality." When I started adult school, I told my mother and she was very happy. I look like my father. I miss my mom. I felt so good when she hugged me and laughed with me. She is very important in my life. Everything I know she taught me.

نسرین

فامیل من

مادرم زن بسیار قوی و مهربان است. او هشت اولاد به دنیا آورده، او همه ما را بسیار دوست دارد و به همه توجه میکند. وقتیکه کوچک بودیم مادرم برای ما میگفت که « در زندگی تان هیچ وقت دروغ نگویید که دروغ گفتن شخصیت انسان را پایان میاورد». او تعلیم را بسیار دوست دارد، وقتیکه من مکتب کلان سالان را شروع کردم برایش گفتم بسیار خوش شد. من مانند پدر خود هستم. من مادر خود را بسیار دوست دارم. وقتیکه مرا در آغوش میگیرد و همرایم میخندد بسیار احساس خوشی میکنم. او در زندگی من بسیار اهمیت دارد. هرچیزی را که میفهمم از برکت مادرم است.

Nasreen Shirzad

I want to have a beautiful family
in the future and cute children
a happy life with my husband
and children and I would like to
have my own business in the
future.

Rahila Hashimi

My name is Rahila.

I like scarves. I wear scarves at home.

I wear scarves always, always.

My favorite scarf is pink with cream lines with a little bit of
brown.

I like it because it is light and cool.

My cousin who is also my friend

Gave me it as a gift

In Afghanistan.

Rahila Hashimi

I would like to have a beautiful

garden full of beautiful

flowers.

Laila Azad

I like scarves because when I am having a bad hair day I could just put the scarf on when I wake up. I don't have to brush my hair. Also when it's cold it keeps me warm.

Laila Azad

I Am Poem

I am caring and smart

I wonder how people went through things in the past

I hear waterfalls

I see pink and blue clouds

I want a good job

I am caring and smart

I pretend I will finish high school at sixteen

I feel I will be successful in life

I touch the rainbow

I try coloring my drawings

I dream to be an artist

I hope for world peace

I am caring and smart

Scan the QR code on your mobile device to hear an audio recording of this poem on Soundcloud.

Laila Azad

I drew about the present and future. Right now we live in a small one story house in Moreno Valley. We have parts of the house that are broken or don't work. In the future I would like to have a good job that I like so I can buy a better house in New York City or Paris. I would like to live in a three story house and I want my mom to come move in with me. I would like to get her all the things she couldn't buy herself, the diamond ring and ruby jewelry.

Suha Huffaker

Home

The smell of stew in the air, onions,
vegetables, meat
The sound of peace and safety
The warmth of people I love

Lots of work to do. Sometimes stress
Pleasures to be enjoyed together: husband
(favorite tv shows, NPR, British dramas, gathered treasures)

Green life surrounds me with weeds and dead
leaves reminding of change
a feeling of belonging to this Earth

Red flaming sunsets delight
water falls over stones soothing

Kumquats, Meyer lemons, and guavas for my birthday
My giving garden
The freedom I feel watching the birds in flight near me

I love children who visit us

Latifa Badrey

My house is the quiet of the father, mother, grandmother, grandfather. They live together in love, sweetness, honesty, all together and full.

Home is Where I Live:
Children's Writing and Art

Michelle Badrey

My life

Yummy

Home sweet home

Our food

My phone

Electronics

A great state

Music

English

Red, white, blue is the flag

Ice cream

California

Animal

Mursal Sherzad

Mursal's Culture

How I dress…We all dress with long sleeves and we
never wear shorts

Where I live…I live in Afghanistan

What I eat…Beans, sheep, chicken, but we never eat pig

My languages are…Pashto and Farsi

What I play…We play everything and every game

My family is…They are nice, quiet

Mursal Sherzad

My Teacher is helpful, nice, and makes us laugh

Yay that I have a beautiful family

Home means love

Oh! It is amazing to have a family

Mom's love

Everyone in my family is beautiful

Self–Portrait of Mursal Sherzad

Tamana Sadat

Lovely Cultures

How I dress…Women are supposed to wear scarves, jeans, pants, shirts, dresses

Where I live…Afghanistan, America

What I eat…No pig, curry, donuts, ice cream, chicken, rice, and yogurt

My languages are…English, Pashto, and Farsi

What I play…soccer, basketball, cricket

My family is…My family is nice and quiet. My baby sister cries loud

How I celebrate…Eid, birthdays, mosque, play school

What art and music I like…harmony, drawing a heart

Bashir Feraz

Bashir's Culture

How I dress…I put on my clothes

Where I live…I live in America

What I eat…Beans and some other stuff

My languages are…Farsi, English

What I play…I love to play tag!

My family is…Noisy

How I celebrate…My birthday is fun!

What art and music I like…I like musical chairs

Bashir Feraz

My goal is to go to school

Why this is my goal because to learn

I will improve my computer skills

My favorite subject is music

My favorite game is Fortnight

This year I want to go to the beach and swim

Bashir Feraz

I had fun with
Mansoor playing soccer
in school
I learned about
airplanes.
Airplanes could fly
fast.

Self-Portrait of Bashir Feraz

Samiullah Shirzad

My mom helps me
Yes mom makes me feel

Happy my mom
On my table my mom cooks yummy food
My mom cooks
Eat chips

An airplane flying me to America
Malls were so big on my first time when I saw them
Eid is an Afghanistan culture that we celebrate in America
Red, white, blue
LOVE!
The American's flag is red, white, and blue
America is a big place

Self-Portrait of Samiullah Shirzad

Mohammad

My bed

You're cool

Apple trees are healthy

Mango

Eat Apple trees

Rules are America

I like my school

Cookies

A big country

Puria

Mangoes in the refrigerator

Yogurt

Horses on TV

Oranges in trees

Many people are dying because of fighting

Everyday I would play with my cousins or friends

A great state

Music

English

Red color is pretty

Ice cream

Cats are cute

Apple

Spogmy Khan

My favorite ice cream is the rainbow ones

Yummy mangoes

Home is life

Olives

My future is to be a teacher

Everything is fun

Apples

Mosawir

Elephant

Raisins

I love my family

Can

A female girl

Tamana Sadat

My home is fantastic
I've been living here for six months

Home sweet home
Oranges are sweet and juicy
Moms are good
English in California

Apples in America
Moms in America
English in America
Roses in America
Ice cream in America
Cold snow in America
America's fun fair is fantastic

Tamana Sadat

Self Portrait

So, today July 31st 2019 we made self portraits and I drew some stuff. Because those are, will, and always will be my favorite stuff to do. The things were golden retriever puppy or dog, I love them because they are cute, smart, lovable, and great with family and kids. The other thing was science. I chose science because when I grow up I want to be a scientist and when I was little I loved science because it's just so cool because there is science all around us. The last and final thing was basketball and swimming. I like basketball, it's fun and matches my personality. Swimming is very refreshing when it's hot.

Self-Portrait of Tamana Sadat

Tamana Sadat

Academic
A better fifth grader
at school and
get all A's

Social
Play with your
pets and friends

Personal
When I grow up I
want to be a scientist
and get straight A's at
school

Family
Help out in the house
and spend more time
with them and
check the mail boxes
and stuff

Tamana Sadat

Words of Encouragement

My name is Tamana and I want
to reach all my goals. Never give up
and try my best because hard
work always pays off.

Tamana Sadat

So, for today I wanted
to talk about golden retrievers
and how smart, cute,
lovable, and super cuddly
they are very easy to train
and are one of my favorite
breeds.

Zahirullah Shirzad

Helping my brother

On my table my mom cooks yummy food

Mom makes me feel good

Eating chips

Zahirullah Shirzad

I learned how you can feel.
And my favorite subject is
science. My favorite animal is
a turtle

> gravity makes you
> stick to the ground

> We learned about the
> planets. And about
> air. And we did draw
> about ourselves
> and just life.

Padsha Badery

My mom takes me to the game shop

Yikes! I spilled milk

Hat

Ocean

Mango

Eat spaghetti

Padsha Badery

My mom and dad live with me

Yummy food

Home is where I live

Our food

My wifi

Electronics

A great state

My state

English

Red, white, and blue flag

Ice cream

Colorful state

Animals

Padsha Badery

One of my memory is that when I came home from school and I saw my mom made my favorite food, also it smelled so good, I ate food first. The food that my mom cooks is so good. If I be a person that grades the food, I will grade my mom food 5 out of 5 ***** stars.

Asia Sadat

My memory is about my teacher Mrs. Simson. And I love math but I don't understand about math. So she helped me about math. And this time I know math.

Self-Portrait of Asia Sadat

Hosai Dawar

My favorite memory is when my dad took a picture of me when I was 3. It was showing I was eating chips.

Hosai Dawar

Peace

My homeland is full of danger.

How are bad people coming to my country?

My country is full of fear!

A place for everyone to live with Peace and Love.
Mangoes are the best fruit.
Elephants are cool in the zoo.
Riding bikes in the nice air.
In stores there are some good stuff.
Cats are cool running around.
Apples are delicious.

Hosai Dawar

I drew this drawing because it represents my future as an astronomer. The stars represent how much I love space, the spaceship represents how much I watch science videos and that's a lot. I drew this drawing because I want girls to follow their dreams and I want them to do what they love and not be controlled by a boy.

This is what I want girls to do.
Boy: "Go be a teacher."
Girl: "No."

This is what I don't want girls to do.
Boy: "Go be a teacher."
Girl: "Ok."

Self-Portrait of Hosai Dawar

Hosai Dawar

There are three questions I have about space.

Is space the least researched?

Why does space have 0 gravity?

How does the planet stay in place and not fly around?

Elaha Moda

My favorite memory when I think about home is when my mom calls out and no one comes for food. Then she starts yelling at us in person. Then we come.

Food is ready.
Later on...
Hurry and come!!!
I'm coming mom!

Elaha Moda

My mom makes me food and does her best

Yikes she burns her hand just to cook the best food for us

Hope, whenever I am struggling she gives me lots of hope

Oops I made a big mistake on my homework. I ripped it, but my mom takes the blame

My mom is very helpful and I'm very happy to have her

Elaha is my name, a name that is different, a name that my mom and dad picked out, a name that I'm happy about

Airplanes zoom through the sky

Money is all we think of, money, money, money

Engineers build houses everyday, the noise

Respectful people are always good people

In stores it's always good to be respectful

Cherry farms are very tasty

Awesome and nice people always doing good deeds and feel good inside

Salma Sadat

My favorite memory about my home in Afghanistan was
   when we had a pool where me and my sisters swam.

I see that I dipped in the water

I smell the sand in the water

I hear splashing of the water

I feel that I am going to die

I taste the water

Special thing about my memory was that I was playing and
   splashing with my friends and my friend saved me.

Self-Portrait of Salma Sadat

Husna Dawar

One of my favorite memories was when it was my dad's birthday and my mom wanted to put up a surprise party for him and on that day everyone was trying to do something to make him happy. We even went shopping to buy gifts. We bought his vanilla flavor cake and after we finished everything when it was time for him to come we turned off all the lights and surprised him. He did not expect that birthday party so we were very happy that made him happy. After, we cut the cake, we gave him his gifts and he was very thankful that we surprised him with a birthday party.

Husna Dawar*

Homeland

My Homeland
The air thick with dust
Cows roaming the streets,
Flashing lights and loud noises,
Children laughing and playing.
Houses painted in sickening colors
sarees tumbling from the
waists of women.
Amazing, flavorful,
mouthwatering food.
Family and friends,
celebrating festivals color in the sky and all around
Though there are things both good and bad,
I love my homeland and I stand proud.

Husna Dawar

Smiley faces

My hometown is Kabul
You can always do what you want to do in life
That is what they taught us

Home is where you live
faces full of happiness and joy
More and more
Eat so you can live
speak so u can love yourself

Keep your words to yourself
Animals can be fun
Beautiful sisters can be by your side
Long time no see
Eyes can be blind
But do your best
Smiley faces :)

Husna Dawar

Things I Like the Most

I like many things. They are fun to think about, watch, and do. Animals that are like bunnies, mostly the white ones, they are just cute and fun to watch. The sport that I like the most is tennis. Not long ago, I never imagined myself holding a racket, but now here I am learning how to play. Not only the sport but also the people I am with, the people that I play tennis with just makes things different. I see them as my second family and I always want to remember them.

Maryam Sherzad

My goal is to be a doctor

Why this is my goal, to be like daddy

I will improve my writing

My favorite subject is music

My favorite game is tag

This year I want to go to Afghanistan

Mansoor Noori

Mansoor's Culture

How I dress…Skull shirt, pants, shoes, and gloves with spikes

Where I live…Person holding gun-like object beneath brown, red, and green flag

What I eat…dollar signs, steaming pizza

My languages are…Farsi

What I play…Silver surfers

My family is…Mom, dad, me, and my sister

How I celebrate…Eid

Mansoor Noori

My goal is to go to school

Why this is my goal, to be smart because I went

I will improve math, writing

My favorite subject is math subject

My favorite game is tag

This year I want to go to the beach

Mansoor Noori

I had fun with the teacher!
They help me out a lot. We
drew. My best friend Bashir
had fun with me, it was fun!
My drawing was funny. My friends
laughed and laughed! We had fun!

Mansoor Noori

I am Mansoor and I believe
in myself I will challenge
myself into a different person
a good person!

Mansoor Noori

Personal

To be good at soccer

and be nice.

Family

To take care of my baby sis!

Academic

Be good at math!

Social

To play for one hour

to make friends.

Mansoor Noori

I will make a potion that will infect the bear into Ender Slender.

Mansoor Noori

Mom helping me

Young siblings in my house are kind

Helping my dad get ready for work

On my table my mom and dad cook me yummy food

My mom makes me feel happy

Eating my dad's food and my mom's

Airplane flying me to America

Malls were so big on my first time when I saw them

Eid is an Afghanistan culture that we celebrate in America

Rabbits are so good to keep

Ice skating is so fun in America

Cat in the Hat is one of the most good movies

America is a good place to live

Self–Portrait of Mansoor Noori

Dewa Feraz

Hi my name is Dewa. Today I am going to tell you guys what I did in class. First we played games and then we drew and then recess and then we came back and we ate.

Dewa Feraz

Today we had such a fun time
all day. We all went to
recess. Today me and my
friends had a great day.
The best day ever,
me and my friends.
We eat, play, draw, write.

Dewa Feraz

A grade is something that makes you up or down.

The English makes you fit in.

U.F.O.

Suhil Sadat

There is something that holds you on the Earth.

Aliens eat their food from

killing animals.

Suhil Sadat

I can learn from my mistakes

I can take a break and come back to it

Suhil Sadat

Academic

to help school

clean

Social

I really like

to hang out

with my friend

Personal

to be good at basketball

Family

to take care of

my baby sis

Suhil Sadat

Rainbow

Red sweet as honey, ladybugs, apples, free as a

Orange cloudy as fall, pumpkins, also the name of

Yellow sands of the beach, bananas, bright as the sun

Green as the leaves, kiwis, wild as a jungle

Blue my favorite color, the gorgeous ocean

Purple, lavender, grapes, vibrant

Self-Portrait of Suhil Sadat

Tabasum Noori

I had fun with the teacher and the best part is drawing. Another one, I love teachers. The best best part is I love pipe cleaners.

Tabasum Noori

I am proud of myself

I matter

Tabasum Noori

My goal is to get straight fours.

My goal is to get a bowl of ice cream.

Tabasum Noori

My goal is to help my mom with cleaning the house.

My goal is to practice soccer.

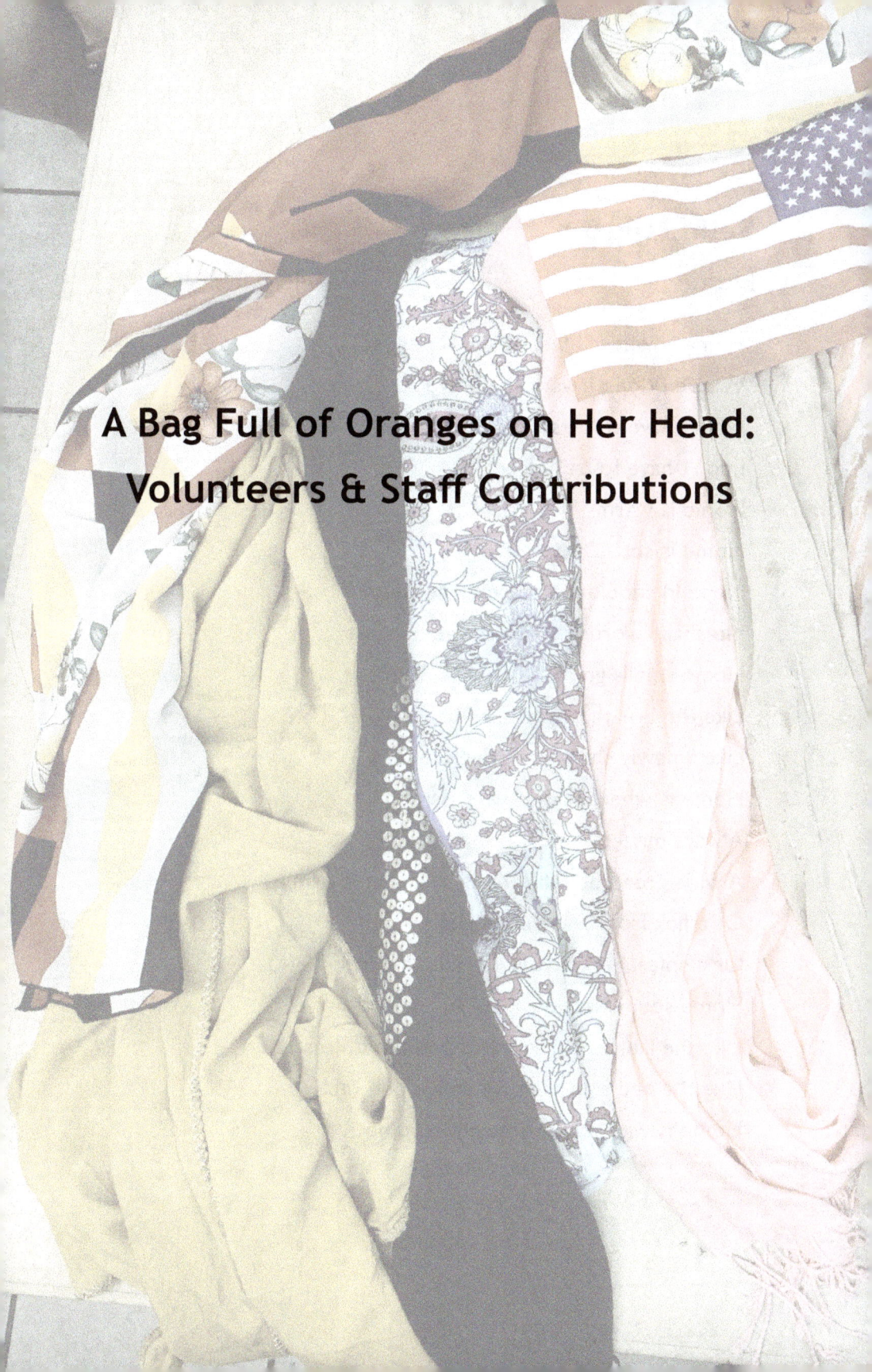

A Bag Full of Oranges on Her Head:
Volunteers & Staff Contributions

Selin Nielsen

Home

Home is where I feel myself the most
Where I don't have to be brave
I don't have to be strong
I don't have to be judged
Home is warm
Home is soft
No cold shoulder from your neighbor
No sharp words that pierce your heart
Home smells good
Like the breath of your newborn
Like a newly showered cheek to kiss
Home is where I am always wanted
Always missed
Always greeted with eyes sparkling and a smile
Or a lick from your furry friend
Or a soft jump on your lap with a purr
Home sounds good
Like the laughter that leaves you breathless
Like the bed squeaking when jumped on
Home is where I am always welcome

Shawni Jones

Sam

You are beautiful my dear friend because...

You are an advocate.

You make time for others.

You live with a vision and purpose.

You listen.

You give love in all its forms.

You notice the details.

You have the most infectious smile.

You are amazing.

Samantha (Sam) Ochse

Shawni

You're beautiful because…

You always find joy in the little things

(like taking a hike or making yummy bread)

You're beautiful for the way you extend kindness to others
even yourself.

I admire the way you honor and celebrate your body and all
of the things it is capable of doing.

Your smile is beautiful and so is the way you faithfully lean
into the gifts and talents you have been given.

You're beautiful because you teach me so much about ser-
vice and bringing hope to other people's lives.

You're more than beautiful. You're radiant, hilarious, a patient
listener, and an extender of grace.

You emulate an unparalleled beauty from within.

Thanks for being unapologetically you!!

Sherry MacKay

Something Magical

And like that it started
>with 4
>with the intention to teach English

I tried to confine you to lessons
but you knew that you needed
>each other

And the rest of you followed
>often timid and cautious
>of us
>and unsure of yourselves

But you were reassured
>by each other
>>because they (your friends) understood
>>they had been there
>>and now
>>it was getting better

But this was not enough
Your community needed to expand
New friends wanted to welcome you
Wanted to do this for you
>came

At first taken aback
Because unlike any other class
>We cried

We prayed

We loved

We laughed

We celebrated

Always with acceptance

And gradually a shift occurred

It just wasn't for you

It was for us

We all needed the purity

of expression

that we learned from you

We became family

So today is not about good-byes
But it is about change
It is about space
To grow
For each of us

The love will not allow a break
It seems like this is bigger than any one of us
So we'll continue to come together
And to create
opportunities
memories
and peace in our hearts

Cati Porter

for Nikia

You are beautiful because your words are not just lovely but
    sweet,

your words are work and your life is work and all that you
    do is always for everyone except yourself—you are the
    endless pot feeding us all and we are so very hungry,

so greedy, and yet you keep feeding us and we fill up, which, I
    hope, feeds you too.

You are beautiful because you matter

and still you are here giving to us and your gift

is the sky in the lake reflecting the trees

that grace the surface

and we are all connected and you

Nikia Chaney

for Cati

    You listen, you take one step back your eyes open and you take it all in as the body is a cup or the head a basket opening woven in silk thread. The words of others the wind the way people move like tides a collection of material that you grasp and shift your own shape around. This is beauty that mutability that patience and turn that generosity that water so soft it can seep past crevices and so strong it can wear down stone. So I wonder if you ever still ever stop to hear the music you make in everything you are. It's like a bell somewhere far away or a drum so low the bones shake and a singing like a chorus, like that good, you singing as if no one could hear.

Nikia Chaney

I sit in a room of beauty, like stars or trees they shine with joy in the friendships they've created. I see one smile ignite like a burst of sunlight and spread and spread until the room glows in gold. How rich we have become how honored we are to witness and bathe such stunning joy.

Nikia Chaney

Landay Poem

I was a stranger in this land

Then you came closer

with open arms and a full plate

So now I take your hand

Yasmin Santos Amaral

Julie

You are beautiful because...

    you bring light wherever you are

    you care about everything and everyone

    even things nobody cares about.

When I think about the word "Patience"

I can see you in my mind

because Patience could be your middle name.

You are beautiful because you make the people around you
    feel beautiful.

Your love and care can change the world like it changed my
    small world.

Now that I know you

I realized that either you are born a Julie

or you have a Julie in your life

because the world is not prepared for so much beauty.

Julie Weatherford

Yasmin

You are beautiful because of...

 your courage

 to travel so far from home to be with us

 to learn a new language and a new culture

 to leave all that is familiar to you to come serve where all
is new to you

 to be so open to try new things

 your gift of yourself

 to serve the homeless

 to care for Afghani children

 to join in the life of your host family and host church

 your love

 to follow Jesus' way of love for the other

 to care about so many other people

 to smile and laugh so easily

 to engage with others looking at people in the eye.

Sherry MacKay

For Zia

Here in my new home

Nobody mothers me like Zia

Secretly, she hands me a dish of food that

    she knows I love

She brings tea for the class but she makes me

    and everyone she serves feel like she's brought it specially
    for them

She brings her tea…her food

    When she presents it, she delivers it with

    the biggest loving smile

When she smiles, when she expresses her

    love for me, for her friends, for her family

I feel like she can love the world

We all want to be mothered by Zia

Sherry MacKay

For Ziagul

When Ziagul walks with a bag full of oranges on her head
I feel like she can balance everything in life
She has the inner strength
the fortitude
the vision
   to move forward
     one step at a time
       with a mischievous smile
         ready to work
          ready to learn
           ready to laugh

Kathy Gómez

My father is the strongest man I know.

He had eight children and provided for all.

He would catch me as a child when I would trip.

But now as an adult I'll be there when he may fall.

I have the appearance of my mother,

Skin like copper and hair like grape vines,

But I have the personality of my father,

quiet like a breeze but strong as a mountain.

Sherry MacKay

My father quietly opened his home

   and opened his heart

   to his new family

   He welcomed his mother-in-law and

      five brother-in-laws who were boys

      into his home

My father quietly made friends

   with those who didn't always have friends

My father quietly teased, sang, made others

   laugh and feel loved

Christina Guillén

Spiders in their Country

There is a big woolly spider in our classroom. I am afraid to touch her, but I don't want her to get hurt. While I look for a cup to carry her outside with, a woman with her head covered stands up. With one hand, she grabs the spider and walks outside.

They say spiders in their country are not mean. They accept and respect them. They say poison makes them afraid and mean.

The women know about poison, but I'm here to tell how the students in this class are diamonds cut in such a way that they shine in all directions like spiderwebs connecting everything, everywhere.

Christina Guillén

Sacred Class

The classroom is a sacred place where the broken pieces can come back.

The women's authenticity makes it easy to breathe.

Their light sings to the surface with shining smiles and sparkling eyes, reminding me.

Zia makes five-star Afghan food on a Wednesday and gives it away.

In the classroom, the women build a mosque. Their tears send golden spires to the sky. The smiles in their eyes lay colorful tile. Their laughter forms strong walls. Their warmth curls the air with incense smoke. Their gentleness is the sweet melody of prayer.

The children's silliness and wonder play like flower petals in the east. They say it's okay not to know. It's okay to pander in the dark, a world of adventure! Now, I remember.

"Best day ever!" they shout on the playground, their laughter like sun melting frost.

Dearness is their fearlessness, joyousness their courage.

Humble students and wise teachers, all of them, learning by their giving.

artwork by Candace

ABOUT INLANDIA INSTITUTE

Inlandia Institute is a regional literary non-profit and publishing house. We seek to bring focus to the richness of the literary enterprise that has existed in this region for ages. The mission of the Inlandia Institute is to recognize, support, and expand literary activity in all of its forms in Inland Southern California by publishing books and sponsoring programs that deepen people's awareness, understanding, and appreciation of this unique, complex and creatively vibrant region.

The Institute publishes books, presents free public literary and cultural programming, provides in-school and after school enrichment programs for children and youth, holds free creative writing workshops for teens and adults, and boot camp intensives. In addition, every two years, the Inlandia Institute appoints a distinguished jury panel from outside of the region to name an Inlandia Literary Laureate who serves as an ambassador for the Inlandia Institute, promoting literature, creative literacy, and community. Laureates to date include Susan Straight (2010-2012), Gayle Brandeis (2012-2014), Juan Delgado (2014-2016), Nikia Chaney (2016-2018), and Rachelle Cruz (2018-2020).

To learn more about the Inlandia Institute, please visit our website at www.InlandiaInstitute.org.

ABOUT GLOCALLY CONNECTED

Glocally Connected is a nonprofit, humanitarian organization established in 2015 to support refugee populations, both globally and locally.

Our organization provides assistance to families that are refugees, that is according to United Nations, people unable to return to their home country because of a well-founded fear of persecution due to their race, membership in a particular social group, political opinion, religion, or national origin. We provide resources such as English-language instruction, employment assistance, and psycho-social support. Glocally Connected provides these services and promotes community building, civic engagement, and human rights awareness in order to support refugees as they adjust to life outside of their country of origin and integrate into their host society. We also advocate on behalf of refugees worldwide on various humanitarian projects.

Glocally Connected does not and shall not discriminate on the basis of race, color, religion (creed), gender, gender expression, age, national origin (ancestry), disability, marital status, sexual orientation, or military status, in any of its activities or operations.

ABOUT SCIPP

(Students and Coyotes Instruction in Poetry and Prose)

SCIPP is a creative partnership between California State University San Bernardino students and educational and nonprofit partners in the region. SCIPP was developed by CSUSB Award-Winning Professor Juan Delgado and Manuel A. Salinas Elementary Master Teachers William Beshears and Larry Light and is currently under the coordination of CSUSB Professor Kelly (KL) Straight Dortch, Liberal Studies Programs Coordinator, Department of English Faculty, SCIPP Charter Member and Coordinator.

Other Inlandia Books

Care: Stories by Christopher Records

San Bernardino, Singing, by Nikia Chaney

Facing Fire: Art, Wildfire, and the End of Nature in the New West by Douglas McCulloh

Writing from Inlandia: Work from the Inlandia Creative Writing Workshops, an annual anthology

In the Sunshine of Neglect: Defining Photographs and Radical Experiments in Inland Southern California, 1950 to the Present by Douglas McCulloh

Henry L. A. Jekel: Architect of Eastern Skyscrapers and the California Style by Dr. Vincent Moses and Catherine Whitmore

Orangelandia: The Literature of Inland Citrus by Gayle Brandeis

While We're Here We Should Sing by The Why Nots

Go to the Living by Micah Chatterton

No Easy Way: Integrating Riverside Schools - A Victory for Community by Arthur L. Littleworth

www.ingramcontent.com/pod-product-compliance
Lightning Source LLC
Chambersburg PA
CBHW051527050726
47503CB00014B/2053